SPACE
TRAVEL

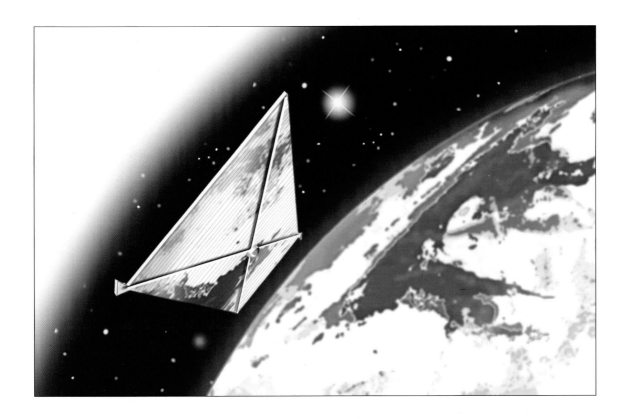

MIKE GOLDSMITH

RAINTREE
STECK-VAUGHN
PUBLISHERS

A Harcourt Company

Austin   New York
www.steck-vaughn.com

SPACE TRAVEL

Other titles in the series: • Comets and Asteroids • Constellations • The Earth • The Moon • The Solar System • Space Mysteries • The Sun

Published by Raintree Steck-Vaughn Publishers, an imprint of Steck-Vaughn Company

Library of Congress Cataloging-in-Publication Data
Goldsmith, Mike.
Space travel / Mike Goldsmith.
    p.   cm.—(Spinning through space)
    Includes bibliographical references and index.
    ISBN 0-7398-2744-8
    1. Manned space flight—Juvenile literature.
    2. Interplanetary voyages—Juvenile literature.
    3. Space colonies—Juvenile literature.
    [1. Space flight. 2. Manned space flight.
    3. Outer space—Exploration]
    I. Title. II. Series.
    TL873 .G63   2001
    629.45—dc21   00-042458

Printed in Italy. Bound in the United States.
1 2 3 4 5 6 7 8 9 0 05 04 03 02 01

CONTENTS

ESCAPE FROM EARTH

The space mission was in trouble. There had been communication problems, the spaceship was going too fast, and now the alarm was buzzing, warning that the computer was overloaded.

The first story of a journey to the moon was written about A.D. 160. Instead of a rocket-powered spaceship, the moon was reached by means of a sailing ship—and a very strong wind!

The spaceship was the *Eagle*, and its mission was to take American astronauts Neil Armstrong and Buzz Aldrin to the moon, a place where no human had ever been.

Looking down at the lunar landscape rushing by below, Armstrong saw that they were off course and heading straight toward a mass of boulders—if he didn't do something, their voyage would end with a spectacular crash.

◀ The *Eagle* approaches the moon. The Earth is in view over the lunar horizon.

On the moon, things are six times lighter than on Earth. The ladder the first astronauts climbed down from their spaceship would have broken under their weight, if they had been on Earth.

▲ Buzz Aldrin climbs down the ladder of the *Eagle* to become the second person (after Neil Armstrong) to set foot on the moon.

The *Eagle* Lands

Armstrong knew what he had to do. He took over control from the computer and diverted the spaceship's course. But the landing site he chose was also covered with boulders, and he had almost no fuel left. His next choice had to be his last. If it was wrong, he would die on the moon, hundreds of thousands of miles from home. He changed the path of the spacecraft once more— and saw a clear space at last. With fewer than 30 seconds of fuel remaining, he eased the *Eagle* down to the moon's surface. The rockets scattered dust that hadn't moved in a million years. The date was July 20, 1969, and people had landed on another world.

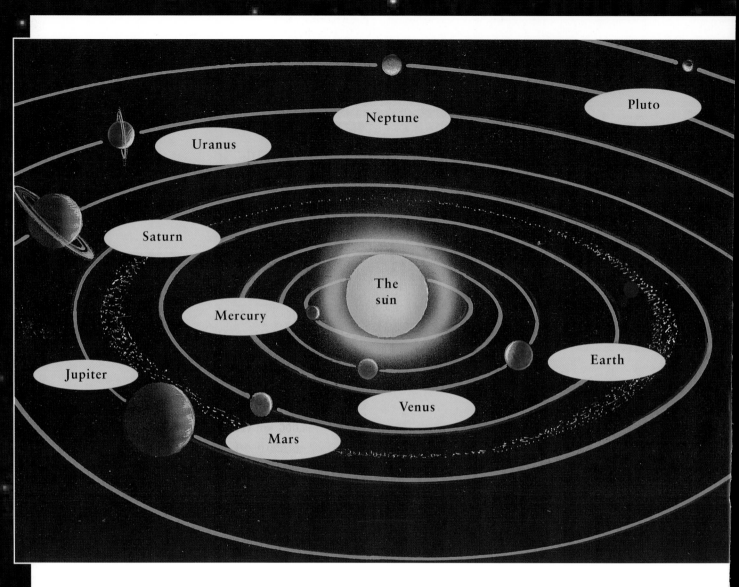

▲ The sun and planets of the solar system (not to scale)

If the sun suddenly exploded, we would not see it happen until the light reached the Earth, more than eight minutes later. Until then we would still see the sun shining normally in the sky.

The Solar System

Space is vast. The nearest destination for a spacecraft is the moon—more than 217,485 mi. (350,000 km) away. If there was a road to the moon and a car drove along it at 62 mi. (100 km) per hour, it would take more than four months to get there!

The rockets that carried the astronauts to the moon took just three days.

Space Distances

Scientists sometimes measure the huge distances to planets or stars by the time light takes to get there. Light travels at the incredible speed of over a billion miles per hour. It could go around the world seven times in one second.

A light second is the distance light travels in a second, or 186,400 mi. (300,000 km), and a light-year is the distance light travels in a year, or 5.87 trillion mi. (9.46 trillion km).

If you imagine the Earth as the size of a marble, the nearest star would be 18,640 mi. (30,000 km) away.

Our neighbors	Closest Distance
The moon	221,200 mi./356,000 km (1.2 light seconds)
The planet Venus	23,600,000 mi./38,000,000 km (2.1 light minutes)
The sun	91,400,000 mi./147,000,000 km (8.2 light minutes)
Proxima Centauri (the nearest star)	24,800,000,000,000 mi./ 40,000,000,000,000 km (4.2 light-years)

Although the distances to the other planets in the solar system are huge, spacecraft from Earth have visited all of them except Pluto. Some have now traveled billions of miles from Earth and are beyond the farthest planet and on their way to the stars.

◄ The *Voyager 2* space probe passing Neptune in 1989. The sun can be seen 2.8 billion mi. (4.5 billion km or more than 4 light-hours) away.

FIRST STEPS TO SPACE

Rocket Technology

Rockets work by burning fuel that releases a jet of gases to push the rocket forward. There are two types of rocket fuel—solid and liquid.

Solid fuel rockets were invented in China hundreds of years ago and are still used as fireworks. But rockets that take people into space burn liquid fuels. All rocket fuel needs oxygen to burn. Because rockets have to travel through space where there is no oxygen, they take their own supply with them in liquid form.

The *Saturn V* had fuel tanks that were so well insulated that an ice cube placed in them would take eight years to melt!

▶ This *Saturn V* rocket, launched on July 16, 1969, resulted in the first manned lunar landing.

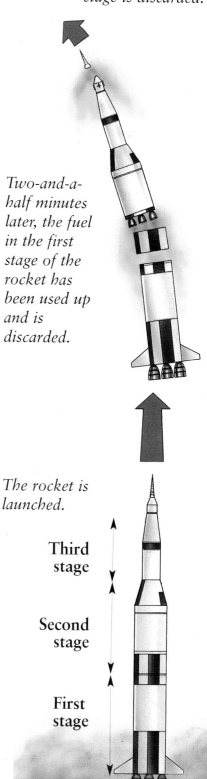

Eight-and-a-half minutes after launch, the second stage is discarded.

Rockets work quite differently than planes. A plane uses the air to help it fly, but a rocket is pushed forward by a jet of hot gases produced by burning fuel. Air just gets in the way of rockets—they move more easily in space. Most of the fuel of a rocket is used to escape from the pull of the Earth's gravity.

Once the rocket has reached a speed called the escape velocity, it is traveling fast enough to escape from the Earth without burning more fuel. The Earth's escape velocity is 6.95 mi. (11.2 km) per second; hundreds of times faster than a firework rocket can travel.

The *Saturn V* rocket that took astronauts to the moon burned almost 13 tons of fuel every second when it was launched.

Two-and-a-half minutes later, the fuel in the first stage of the rocket has been used up and is discarded.

The rocket is launched.

Third stage

Second stage

First stage

The lighter a rocket is, the less fuel it needs. To reduce the weight of space rockets, sections are allowed to drop off once the fuel they contain has been used up. Rockets like these are called stage-rockets.

▶ The *Saturn V* was a rocket over 360 ft. (110 m) tall with the *Apollo* modules installed at the top.

▲ The launch of one of
Robert Goddard's rockets in 1937

The First Rockets

The liquid-fuel rocket was invented in 1903 by a Russian scientist, Konstantin Tsiolkovsky, who also developed the theory of the stage rocket.

The first launch of a liquid-fuel rocket took place on March 16, 1926 from a farm in Massachusetts. The rocket wasn't very big, and it only reached a height of 41 ft. (12.5 m), but it marked a turning point in rocket history. Its inventor was Robert Goddard, an American physicist.

Bigger rockets called V2s were developed in Germany by Wernher von Braun during World War II. After the war, von Braun worked in the United States building space rockets.

In 1968, Russian tortoises flew around the moon before returning safely to Earth in the *Zond 5* spaceship.

◄ The *V2* was developed in Germany under the technical direction of von Braun. On its way to attack London in 1944, a *V2* left the Earth's atmosphere and became the first spaceship.

The First Satellites

In October 1957, people all over the world tuned in to hear a strange beeping sound from their radios. The signals came from a satellite named *Sputnik 1* that the U.S.S.R. had launched into space. The space age had begun. The next year, the *Juno 1* rocket put *Explorer 1*, America's first satellite, into orbit. *Explorer 1* discovered that near the Earth there are regions filled with radiation that would be deadly to unprotected space travelers. These are called Van Allen belts and are formed by the Earth's magnetism, which traps particles from the sun.

▲ The first satellite, *Sputnik 1*, was launched in 1957.

Thousands of satellites are now in orbit around the Earth. They do all sorts of jobs, from monitoring the weather to relaying television programs.

The First Space Travelers

Soon after *Sputnik 1*, the Russians sent the first traveler into orbit—a dog named Laika, on *Sputnik 2*. The Americans soon sent animals into space, too, including a chimpanzee named Ham. These animal astronauts showed that it would be possible for people to survive space travel.

▲ Space-traveling chimpanzee Ham accepts an apple soon after returning to Earth.

SPACE PEOPLE

Orbiting the Earth

In 1961, a 27-year-old Russian pilot named Yuri Gagarin made history by escaping from the Earth's atmosphere and becoming the first human space traveler. He orbited the Earth once before returning home. He was soon followed by others. Valentina Tereshkova became the first woman in space in 1963. Alexei Leonov was the first person to leave his spacecraft and walk in space—protected by a spacesuit.

▲ Russian space-traveler Yuri Gagarin, the first person to travel in space

The first American astronaut to be blasted into space was Alan Shepard, in 1961. He spent just 15 minutes in space before dropping down into the Atlantic Ocean. The next year, astronaut John Glenn was launched into space and made three orbits of the Earth in less than five hours.

◄ American astronaut John Glenn boards his *Mercury* spaceship in 1962.

When their *Voskhod 2* spaceship returned to Earth 1,865 mi. (3,000 km) off course in 1965, and landed in a forest, Russian astronauts had to cope with a pack of hungry wolves.

Journeys to the Moon

In 1965, on a U.S. space mission, one of the astronauts became famous—and got into trouble—for giving the other a corned beef sandwich he had smuggled aboard!

After rockets had become powerful enough to break away from the Earth's gravity, the moon became the next goal of space exploration. In 1961, the United States committed itself to landing a person on the moon by 1970.

In 1965 and 1966, ten manned *Gemini* spacecraft were launched, to get astronauts ready for moon journeys. The astronauts practiced space walking and found out how living in space affected them. They learned how to fly spaceships and even how to join them together in space.

◄ Buzz Aldrin leaves *Gemini 12,* as part of his training for landing on the moon.

13

LIVING IN SPACE

Life in space is difficult and dangerous. There is no air to breathe, so spacecraft have to take their own supplies with them. The lack of air also means that special protection is needed from the deadly radiation of the sun. Also any places that are in the shade are bitterly cold.

Astronauts can only leave their spacecraft wearing spacesuits that protect them from the airlessness, radiation, and extreme temperatures in space.

Valerij Poliyakov spent a record 437 days aboard the *Mir* space station.

▼ Astronauts in the airlock of the *Discovery* space shuttle, on its way to the Russian space station *Mir* in 1995.

▲ In the weightless environment of the *Mir* space station, crew members of two spacecraft meet.

In modern spacecraft, all these problems have been overcome, but there is one thing that astronauts still have to cope with—weightlessness. In space, there is no up or down, and people and things float. You can't drink a cup of tea in space, because the tea would just float out of the cup. You have to suck it through a straw instead.

Weightlessness causes all sorts of changes in people. They can grow several centimeters taller, and, unless they do special exercises, their muscles shrink and their bones weaken. Many space travelers also suffer from space sickness, which is like air sickness. Luckily it soon wears off.

The longest space walk took 8 hours and 29 minutes. It happened in 1992, when shuttle astronauts had to grapple with a faulty satellite.

FROM THE EARTH TO THE MOON

When the exploration of space began, Russia and America were fierce rivals, and each tried to outdo the other. In particular, both countries were eager to win the space race to the moon.

Many people thought the Russians would win. In 1959, they managed to put the first piece of Earth equipment on the moon, when they crashed a rocket called *Luna 2* there.

In the same year, *Luna 3* flew behind the moon, and photographs were taken of something that no one had ever seen—the moon's far side that is never turned toward the Earth.

▲ The far side of the moon, which cannot be seen from Earth

The astronauts who traveled in *Apollo 10* to go around the moon broke all human speed records. They traveled at 24,800 mi. (39,897 km) per hour—more than 33 times the speed of sound.

More unmanned explorations followed, both by U.S. and Russian spacecraft. A series of U.S. *Ranger* spacecraft sent back spectacular close-ups of the lunar surface before they crashed onto it. But the Russian *Luna 9* was the first craft to land safely on the moon, and *Luna 10*—also Russian—was the first to orbit it. But in the end, the Americans won the race to be first to land people there.

Teflon is a material that was developed to keep moving parts of spacecraft from sticking together—but it was soon used on Earth too, to make nonstick pans.

Neil Armstrong and Buzz Aldrin stepped out of the *Eagle* in 1969 to become the first people to set foot on the moon. The footprints they made will probably still be there millions of years in the future.

◀ Buzz Aldrin standing on the moon's surface in 1969. Reflected in his visor, Neil Armstrong and the *Eagle* can be seen.

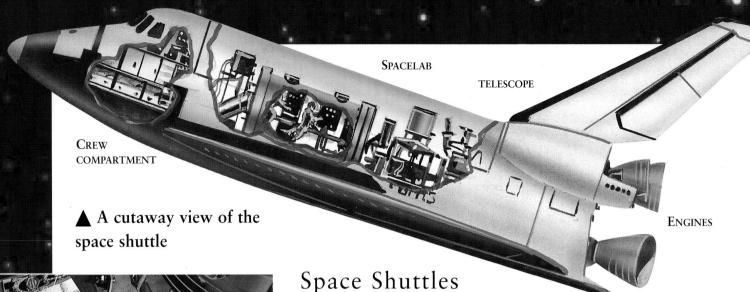

SPACELAB

TELESCOPE

CREW
COMPARTMENT

ENGINES

▲ A cutaway view of the
space shuttle

▲ A full-size model of
the Russian *Salyut 1*
space station

Space Shuttles

The rockets that took people to the
moon were enormous—and very expensive.
And they could only be used once. Something
cheaper was needed that could be used over and
over again, so, in the 1970s, the United States built
the first space shuttle. Space shuttles are now used
regularly, to launch and repair satellites, for
military missions, and for scientific work. But there
have been problems, too. In 1986 the shuttle
Challenger exploded soon after takeoff due to a
gas leak. The whole crew of seven died.

Space Stations

In 1971 a new satellite named *Salyut 1* was sent
into space—but this one was different, because
people could live in it.

Two spiders became famous in 1973 when they learned
to build webs in the weightless environment of the *Skylab* space
station. Their first attempts were a mess, but they got
much better with practice.

Satellites with people onboard are called space stations. The first U.S. space station was *Skylab*, which was launched in 1973 and stayed in space until 1979, when it crashed back to Earth.

In 1869, a magazine published the first story about a space station—made of bricks! The story was *The Brick Moon* by E. E Hale.

The Russian space station *Mir* was launched in 1986 and was in use for over ten years. A new International Space Station is being built in orbit around the Earth—a joint venture by the United States, Japan, Canada, Europe, and Russia. The structure will have six laboratories and living accommodations.

▼ The International Space Station will be powered by 43,060 sq. ft. (4,000 sq. m) of solar panels and will accommodate six crew members at a time.

SPACE MISSIONS

Sending people into space is very expensive, because of all the life-support equipment that needs to go with them. So there have been no manned moon landings since 1972, and the space probes that have traveled beyond the moon have not had people on onboard.

Each rocket that took astronauts to the moon burned up enough fuel to fill an Olympic swimming pool. But once a spacecraft is on its way and has escaped from the Earth's gravity, it will keep on going until it either crashes into something or is pulled down by the gravity of another planet. This is because, in space, there is no air to slow down the spaceship.

▲ The giant planet Neptune, photographed by the *Voyager 2* probe in 1989. A storm system, called the Great Dark Spot, can be seen on the left, with bright white clouds nearby.

The theory of gravitation was used to find the planet Neptune in 1846. Astronomers had noticed that Uranus was not moving through space quite as they expected. They thought the gravitational pull of an unknown planet might be responsible and found Neptune where they predicted it should be.

▶ The "slingshot effect" was used by *Voyager 2* to explore the outer solar system. By passing close to Jupiter, the space probe used the gravity of the giant planet to increase its speed and steer it toward Saturn, Uranus, and Neptune.

When the "slingshot effect" is used to speed up a spacecraft, the planet slows down—by an amount less than a millionth of a millionth of a millimeter per second!

By steering a spacecraft near a planet, it is possible to use the planet's gravity to help speed it up. This is called the "slingshot effect." There was a stroke of luck for space explorers in the 1970s. They realized that the four giant planets, Jupiter, Saturn, Uranus, and Neptune, would soon be lined up. This meant it was possible to use the "slingshot effect" to send spacecraft such as *Pioneer* and *Voyager* on grand tours to see them all. Alignments like this happen only every 180 years.

EXPLORING THE PLANETS

Unmanned space probes have led the way in the exploration of the solar system.

Venus

The first successful probe to another planet was *Mariner 2*, which flew past the planet Venus in 1962. Space probes that venture inside the atmosphere of Venus are soon melted and crushed by the intense heat and pressure. But some have managed to land and send back photographs of the surface before they were destroyed.

Mars

Mariner 4 flew past Mars in 1965, taking photographs that showed that Mars had a moonlike surface. In 1976, two American *Viking* craft landed there and sent back pictures of the rocky landscape.

Mariner 1 was a probe that was supposed to go to Venus. It went off course and had to be destroyed—because a dash had been left out of its computer's coded instructions!

▲ Mars, photographed by the *Viking 1* spacecraft. The giant volcano Olympus is visible at the top right. Three more volcanoes can be seen at center right.

In 1997, the *Pathfinder* mission carried a small robot rover to Mars to travel across the rough surface of the planet.

Mercury

In 1974, *Mariner 10* flew past Mercury, the closest planet to the sun. It sent back the first images of its surface—covered with craters like those on the moon.

The Outer Planets

In the 1970s, *Pioneer 10*, *Pioneer 11*, *Voyager 1*, and *Voyager 2* were launched on missions to visit the outer planets (Jupiter, Saturn, Uranus, and Neptune) and their moons. The *Galileo* probe later visited Jupiter, venturing inside the thick atmosphere of the planet for the first time.

Pictures and video disks are included in several space probes, as messages to any aliens they may encounter.

◀ *Pioneer 10* reaches **Jupiter in 1973. The intense radiation from the planet almost destroyed the space probe's instruments.**

FUTURE VOYAGES

Saturn

 The *Cassini* spacecraft approaches Titan. The dish-shaped object on the left is the *Huygens* probe.

In 1997, the American *Cassini* spacecraft set off on a journey to Saturn, to arrive there in 2004. In addition to cameras to photograph the giant planet, its rings, and its moons, *Cassini* carried a European probe, known as *Huygens. It was* designed to parachute down through the atmosphere of Titan, Saturn's biggest moon.

Mars

For a manned mission to Mars, a whole series of spaceships is planned. The first craft will carry supplies and equipment for the human explorers who will arrive later, after traveling through space for at least four months.

Saturn's moon, Titan, is the only one in the solar system with a thick atmosphere. It contains chemicals like those found in the fumes from car exhaust.

On Mars, things weigh only a third as much as they do on Earth, years are nearly twice as long, and the sky is pink.

▼ The proposed Pluto-Kuiper Express space probe passes near the planet Pluto. Pluto's huge moon, Charon, can be seen in the upper left of the picture.

Once they are there, they will probably stay for more than a year, looking for hidden water supplies, searching for traces of life, and making their own fuel, oxygen, and water from materials found on Mars itself. This mission will be extremely expensive, and no date for it has yet been set.

Pluto and Beyond

Pluto, the outermost planet in the solar system, is the only one never to have been visited by a spacecraft. But there are plans to send a probe to Pluto that might arrive in 2012. The probe would also investigate Pluto's moon, Charon. It might be sent on beyond Pluto to explore some mysterious icy objects that have recently been discovered farther out in space.

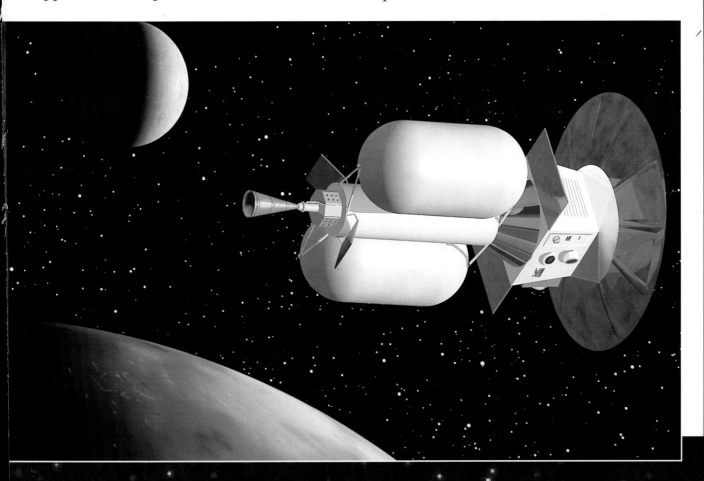

SPACESHIPS OF TOMORROW

So far, spaceships have been powered by rockets that burn liquid fuels, sometimes helped by gravity. But liquid fuels are heavy and expensive, and gravity can only be used for certain routes through the solar system. So tomorrow's spaceships will need to find other sources of power.

In the 1950s, a spaceship was suggested that would work by exploding atomic bombs behind it—at a rate of five per second!

The Solar Sail

There are plans for a spaceship that won't need to carry its own fuel—it will use the power of the sun instead. The spaceship is called a solar sail because the pressure of the sun's light pushes it through space in the same way the wind pushes a sailing ship through the sea.

▶ **A solar sail drifting above the Earth**

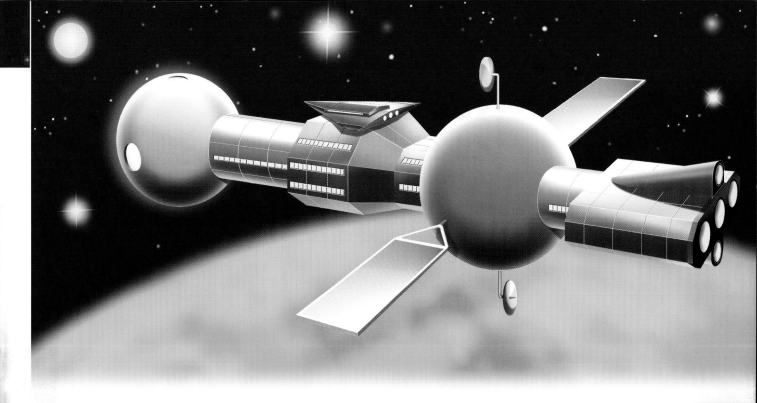

▲ A possible antimatter spaceship of the future, equipped with a shuttle craft to ferry its passengers to the planets it visits. The glow at the front is an energy field used to protect it from meteoroids on its long journeys.

Ion Drive

Ion drives have already been used to maneuver some satellites. In an ion-drive engine, oxygen or other substances are broken down into fragments, called ions, that are charged with electricity. Electromagnets are then used to fire these ions into space. The ions push the spacecraft forward, instead of the burning gases that rockets use.

Antimatter

Antimatter is a substance that looks just like ordinary matter. But, when antimatter and normal matter touch, they destroy each other and an enormous amount of energy is released. Tiny amounts of antimatter are made on Earth even now. It may one day be possible to use it to power spacecraft.

If a piece of antimatter the size of a grain of sand were allowed to touch ordinary matter, enough energy would be released to boil millions of gallons of water.

STARSHIPS

▼ A possible human colony on another planet. The thin, unbreathable atmosphere means that the colony has to be protected by a pressurized dome.

In the distant future, it may be possible for people to travel to other stars.

The Earth will not last forever. In millions of years time, the sun will grow so big that the Earth will either be swallowed up or get so hot that everything on it will be destroyed. Escape to other star systems would require new types of engines. Even then, the journeys are likely to take many years—even centuries!

Many planets orbiting other stars have been found, and more are being discovered each year. So if we ever manage to reach the stars, there may be many new worlds to explore.

▲ A gigantic spaceship of the distant future, capable of crossing the enormous spaces between the stars.

The *Voyager* and *Pioneer* space probes should eventually reach other stars—after journeys lasting more than 80,000 years.

To survive such long journeys through space, people might be put into a deep sleep for a long time by making them very cold. Experiments on animals have shown that this is possible. Automatic systems would wake the space travelers up again, perhaps hundreds of years later. By then, they would be millions and millions of miles from Earth.

People who travel so far would never return to Earth, but they might set up colonies on planets going around other stars, far away in space and time.

GLOSSARY

Antimatter Possible fuel for future spaceships. Pure energy can be converted to equal amounts of matter and antimatter.

Astronaut A person who travels through space.

Atmosphere Layer of gases surrounding the Earth or other planet or moon.

Escape velocity The speed a spaceship must reach to escape from a planet.

Gravity The pull that holds us to Earth and keeps the planets going around the sun.

Ion drive A device that uses a stream of broken-up atoms to push a spacecraft through space.

Light-year The distance that light travels in a year—5.87 trillion miles (9.46 trillion kilometers).

Lunar To do with the moon.

Meteoroids Solid objects, often the remains of comets, that travel through space.

NASA The National Aeronautics and Space Administration, an agency that organizes space exploration on behalf of the U.S. government.

Orbit The path of one object around another.

Satellite An orbiting body; either a moon or an artificial object.

Solar To do with the sun.

Solar sail A device that uses the power of the sun to push it through space.

Solar system The sun and the planets, moons, asteroids, and comets that go around it.

Space probe An unmanned spacecraft sent to explore space.

Space shuttle A reusable spacecraft that carries people and material into space. It is launched by a rocket but lands like a plane.

Space sickness Illness that affects many space travelers.

Space station An artificial satellite that can carry people.

FURTHER INFORMATION

Web sites:

http://ispec.scibernet.com/station/
asteroid.html
Asteroids and Meteoroids

http://www.jpl.nasa.gov/solarsystem/
The Solar System

http://comets.amsmeteors.org
Comets and Meteor Showers

Books to read:

Angliss, Sarah. *Cosmic Journeys: A Beginner's Guide to Space and Time Travel*. Copper Beech Books, 1998.

Cole, Michael D. *Columbia: First Flight of the Space Shuttle*. Enslow, 1995.

Hawcock, David. *The Amazing Pop-Up Space Shuttle*. Dorling Kindersley, 1998.

Johnstone, Michael and Douglas Millard. *The History News: in Space*. Walker Books, 1999.

Stott, Carole. *Moon Landing*. Dorling Kindersley, 1999.

Streissguth, Thomas. *John Glenn*. Lerner, 1999.

Places to visit:

National Air and Space Museum
7th and Independence Ave., S.W.
Washington, D.C. 20560
(202) 357-2700
www.nasm.edu

NASA/Kennedy Space Center
Kennedy Space Center, FL 32899
(407) 452-2121
www.ksc.nasa.gov

INDEX

All numbers in **bold** refer to pictures.

Picture acknowledgments:

The publishers would like to thank the following for allowing their pictures to be reproduced in this book: Bruce Coleman/Astrofoto 8, 16, 29; Eye Ubiquitous *cover*; HWPL 10 (top); Science Photo Library *cover*, 25/David Ducros 24/Victor Habbick 28/David A. Hardy 11 (top), 21/Seth Shostak 7/NASA 14, 19, 20, 22; Popperfoto 4, 5, 10 (bottom), 11 (bottom), 12 (both), 13, 15, 17, 18; Peter Bull Art Studio 2, 26, 27; all other artwork from HWPL.